Junior Bios

Kumail Nanjiani

By Nora Gardiner

Enslow Publishing

Please visit our website, www.enslow.com. For a free color catalog of all our high-quality books, call toll free 1-800-398-2504 or fax 1-877-980-4454.

Library of Congress Cataloging-in-Publication Data

Names: Gardiner, Nora, author.
Title: Kumail Nanjiani / Nora Gardiner.
Description: New York : Enslow Publishing, 2022. | Series: Junior bios | Includes index.
Identifiers: LCCN 2020036888 (print) | LCCN 2020036889 (ebook) | ISBN 9781978525405 (library binding) | ISBN 9781978525382 (paperback) | ISBN 9781978525399 (set) | ISBN 9781978525412 (ebook)
Subjects: LCSH: Nanjiani, Kumail–Juvenile literature. | Actors–United States–Biography–Juvenile literature. | Comedians–United States–Biography–Juvenile literature.
Classification: LCC PN2287.N27 G38 2022 (print) | LCC PN2287.N27 (ebook) | DDC 791.4302/8092 [B]–dc23
LC record available at https://lccn.loc.gov/2020036888
LC ebook record available at https://lccn.loc.gov/2020036889

First Edition

Published in 2022 by
Enslow Publishing
29 E. 21st Street
New York, NY 10010

Designer: Deanna Paternostro
Editor: Kate Mikoley

Photo credits: Cover, p. 1 (Kumail Nanjiani) Jeff Kravitz/Contributor/FilmMagic, Inc/Getty Images; cover, p. 1 (photo frame) Aleksandr Andrushkiv/Shutterstock.com; marble texture used throughout HardtIllustrations/Shutterstock.com; lined paper texture used throughout Mtsaride/Shutterstock.com; watercolor texture used throughout solarbird/Shutterstock.com; p. 5 Gary Gershoff/Contributor/Getty Images Entertainment/Getty Images; p. 7 FilmMagic/Contributor/FilmMagic/Getty Images; p. 9 Rich Fury/Staff/Getty Images Entertainment/Getty Images; p. 11 JEAN-BAPTISTE LACROIX/Contributor/AFP/Getty Images; p. 13 Jason Merritt/Staff/Getty Images Entertainment/Getty Images; p. 15 Mark Sullivan/Contributor/WireImage/Getty Images; p. 17 Chance Yeh/Contributor/FilmMagic/Getty Images; p. 19 Rachel Luna/Stringer/WireImage/Getty Images.

Printed in the United States of America

CPSIA compliance information: Batch #CWENS22: For further information contact Enslow Publishing, New York, New York, at 1-800-398-2504.

Contents

Funny and More 4
Starting Stand-Up 6
The Emily Effect 8
From Writing to Acting 10
TV Time 12
The Big Movie 16
Superhero Kumail 20
Kumail's Timeline 21
Glossary 22
For More Information 23
Index 24

Words in the glossary appear in **bold** type the first time they are used in the text.

Funny and More

Kumail Nanjiani is one of the most special voices in Hollywood today. He's best known for being funny as a **comedian**, writer, and actor. But as a native of Pakistan, Kumail knows the important part he plays in increasing **representation** of Asian Americans in TV shows and movies.

FACTS BEHIND THE FIGURE

Kumail was raised a Shiite Muslim, or follower of the religion, or faith, of Islam.

AT HOME, KUMAIL'S FAMILY SPOKE THE LANGUAGE URDU.

Kumail was born in Karachi, Pakistan. He learned to speak English at school and from American TV shows and movies. He left Pakistan to go to college in Iowa.

Starting Stand-Up

Kumail said that going to school in Iowa was a shock: "I thought, from watching TV and stuff, that America was one place. They only show you L.A. and New York. They don't warn you about Iowa." Until he started college in the late 1990s, Kumail had never seen a **stand-up comedy** special. Then, his last year in college, he did his first stand-up comedy set.

After school, Kumail moved to Chicago, Illinois. He performed stand-up as much as he could.

AT FIRST, KUMAIL DIDN'T TALK ABOUT HIS LIFE OR RELIGION IN HIS STAND-UP SETS. LATER, HE BECAME KNOWN FOR IT.

The Emily Effect

Kumail got a day job so he could perform at night. At one show in 2006, he met Emily V. Gordon. Shortly into the time they were dating, Emily got very sick. Kumail stayed by her side the whole time she was in the hospital. They got married soon after she was well again!

FACTS BEHIND THE FIGURE

Kumail wrote and performed a one-man show called "Unpronounceable" about his life as a Muslim.

*THE TIME EMILY WAS SICK GREATLY **INFLUENCED** KUMAIL'S LIFE. THE STORY OF HER ILLNESS WOULD CHANGE HIS LIFE AGAIN YEARS LATER!*

Kumail's parents had **expected** him to marry a Shiite Muslim woman. Emily is white and non-Muslim. However, his parents learned to love and accept her. Kumail began to look at his past and use it in his work.

From Writing to Acting

Kumail and Emily moved to New York City in late 2007. Kumail appeared in one **sketch** on *Saturday Night Live* and on a few **episodes** of *The Colbert Report*. Then he landed a writing and acting job on a TV show called *Michael & Michael Have Issues*. It only lasted seven episodes.

Kumail decided to try centering in on acting. In 2010, he got a part in a movie, *Life as We Know It*. But it didn't turn out to be his big break.

IN 2009, KUMAIL SOLD A TV SHOW IDEA BASED ON HIS LIFE WITH EMILY TO NBC. THE SHOW WAS NEVER MADE.

TV Time

Kumail did end up on a long-running TV show—a few of them! First, in 2011, he began playing Pindar Singh on *Franklin & Bash*. He later said that was where he really learned how to act. It was also the first time when he was making all his money from a comedy or acting job!

FACTS BEHIND THE FIGURE

Kumail made his first comedy special in 2013. It aired on Comedy Central!

KUMAIL CONTINUED TO WRITE AND DO STAND-UP WHEN HE WASN'T FILMING TV SHOWS.

Kumail also started appearing on episodes of the comedy show *Portlandia* in 2011. The next year, he began voicing Prismo on the cartoon *Adventure Time*.

After three seasons on *Franklin & Bash*, Kumail was ready to move on. He wanted to make a show that was just a comedy. Kumail heard about a new show called *Silicon Valley* that sounded like a "dream job." He **auditioned** for it. The team making the show liked Kumail so much that they wrote a part just for him!

In His Own Words

*"There are very few Muslim characters ... who are just people with **complicated** backstories who do normal things ... we also need Muslim characters who, like, go to Six Flags and eat ice cream."*

WRITERS ON SILICON VALLEY WORKED WITH KUMAIL TO MAKE SURE HIS CHARACTER WAS MORE THAN JUST A ***STEREOTYPE.***

Kumail called being on *Silicon Valley* one of the best experiences of his life. He played Dinesh Chugtai from 2014 to 2019.

The Big Movie

Between shooting *Silicon Valley* and other shows, Kumail was writing with his wife, Emily. They wrote a movie about when they started dating and Emily's illness. *The Big Sick* starred Kumail as a character based on himself. The movie is also about what it's like to be a Muslim in the United States and the conflicts the real Kumail had with his family about their faith.

FACTS BEHIND THE FIGURE

Kumail has appeared on or done voices for many TV shows, including *Community*, *Bob's Burgers*, *The X-Files*, *The Twilight Zone*, and more!

KUMAIL STARRED IN THE BIG SICK WITH ZOE KAZAN. SHE PLAYED EMILY.

Kumail and Emily were **nominated** for an Academy Award for Best Original Screenplay in 2017!

The Big Sick put Kumail in the spotlight—and he stayed there! In 2019, he starred with Dave Bautista in *Stuber*. Kumail felt the action-packed comedy also made an important statement: neither male lead was white! That summer, Kumail also voiced Pawny in *Men in Black: International*.

Over the years, Kumail had been offered parts in comic-book movies and turned them down. He had a dream to not just be in a superhero movie. He wanted to be the superhero! That was about to happen.

IN 2018, KUMAIL WAS NAMED ONE OF *TIME* MAGAZINE'S 100 MOST INFLUENTIAL PEOPLE.

Superhero Kumail

Kumail got the part of Kingo in the Marvel Studios movie *The Eternals*. He decided he really wanted to look like a superhero and spent a year getting very fit!

Kumail and Emily joined forces again to create *Little America* in 2020. The show tells true stories of all kinds of American immigrants, or people who come to a country to live there.

Kumail's success shows just how important unique, creative voices are in entertainment! What will he do next?

In His Own Words

"The stories you see as a kid show you what's possible. I mean, I'm almost 40, and when I saw a brown guy [fighting well] in the new Star Wars movie I started crying in the movie theater."

Kumail's Timeline

1997: KUMAIL MOVES TO THE UNITED STATES TO GO TO COLLEGE.

2007: KUMAIL MARRIES EMILY V. GORDON.

2009: HE WRITES AND APPEARS IN *MICHAEL & MICHAEL HAVE ISSUES.*

2011: KUMAIL BEGINS ACTING ON *FRANKLIN & BASH* AND *PORTLANDIA.*

2014: HE STARTS APPEARING ON *SILICON VALLEY.*

2017: *THE BIG SICK* COMES OUT. KUMAIL AND EMILY ARE NOMINATED FOR AN ACADEMY AWARD.

2018: KUMAIL IS NAMED ONE OF *TIME* MAGAZINE'S MOST INFLUENTIAL PEOPLE.

2019: KUMAIL STARS IN *STUBER.*

2020: *LITTLE AMERICA* COMES OUT.

2021: KUMAIL STARS IN *THE ETERNALS* AS KINGO.

Glossary

audition To try out.

comedian A person whose job is to try to make people laugh.

complicated Hard to understand or explain.

episode A TV show that is one part of a series.

expect To think that something is likely to happen.

influence To have an effect on.

nominate To suggest someone for an honor.

representation The way a TV show, movie, book, or other media deals with and presents age, gender, or ethnicity.

sketch A short, funny skit.

stand-up comedy The performance of jokes or funny stories, commonly while standing alone on a stage or in front of a camera.

stereotype An often unfair and untrue belief people have about all members of a certain group.

For More Information

Books

Bray, Adam. *The Marvel Studios Character Encyclopedia*. New York, NY: DK Publishing, 2019.

Wood, Alix. *Be an Actor: Bring the Script to Life*. New York, NY: PowerKids Press, 2018.

Websites

Do You Have What It Takes to Be a Stand-Up Comedian?
teenkidsnews.com/tkn-news/careers/do-you-have-what-it-takes-to-be-a-stand-up-comedian/
Interested in stand-up comedy? Read this article to find out more about how to get started!

The Eternals
www.marvel.com/comics/discover/1398/the-eternals
Learn more about *The Eternals* comic books.

Publisher's note to educators and parents: Our editors have carefully reviewed these websites to ensure that they are suitable for students. Many websites change frequently, however, and we cannot guarantee that a site's future contents will continue to meet our high standards of quality and educational value. Be advised that students should be closely supervised whenever they access the internet.

Index

Adventure Time, 13
Bautista, Dave, 18, 19
Big Sick, The, 16, 17, 18, 21
Chicago, Illinois, 6
Colbert Report, The, 10
Eternals, The, 20, 21
Franklin & Bash, 12, 14, 21
Gordon, Emily V., 8, 9, 10, 11, 16, 17, 20, 21
Iowa, 5, 6
Islam, 4, 8, 9, 14, 16
Kazan, Zoe, 17
Life as We Know It, 10
Little America, 20, 21
Men in Black: International, 18
Michael & Michael Have Issues, 10, 21
New York City, 6, 10
Pakistan, 4, 5
Portlandia, 13, 21
Saturday Night Live, 10
Silicon Valley, 14, 15, 16, 21
stand-up comedy, 6, 7, 12, 13
Stuber, 18, 21
"Unpronounceable," 8